# DevSecOps for Continuous Innovation

**MOHAMED FAWZI ELGENDI**

WWW.FAWZOOZ.AI

Copyright © 2024 Mohamed Fawzi Elgendi

No part of this work may be reproduced, distributed, transmitted in any form or by any means, including photocopying, recording, or other electronic or mechanical methods, without the prior written permission of the author, except in the case of brief quotations embodied in critical reviews and certain other noncommercial uses permitted by copyright law with the source duly credited. The names, characters, businesses, places, events, locales, and incidents are either the products of the author's imagination or used in a fictitious manner. Any resemblance to actual persons, living or dead, or actual events is purely coincidental.

www.mohamedfawzi.net

# Table of Contents

*Preface* ............................................................................................... *7*

*Introduction to DevSecOps* ............................................................ *11*

*The Culture of DevSecOps* ............................................................. *17*

*Key Practices in DevSecOps* .......................................................... *22*

*Tools and Technologies* .................................................................. *29*

*Implementing DevSecOps* .............................................................. *36*

*Challenges and Solutions* ............................................................... *42*

*Future of DevSecOps* ...................................................................... *48*

*Integrating DevSecOps with Cloud-Native Technologies* ....... *53*

*Conclusion* ....................................................................................... *59*

*Comprehensive Case Study* ........................................................... *63*

*ABOUT THE AUTHOR* .................................................................. *71*

**PREFACE** 2024
WWW.MOHAMEDFAWZI.NET

# DEVSECOPS FOR CONTINUOUS INNOVATION

# **Preface**

Welcome to "DevSecOps for Continuous Innovation", a guide designed to navigate the confluence of development, operations, and security within modern software development environments. As technology evolves at an unprecedented pace, the need for integrated security practices has never been more crucial. This book aims to demystify the concept of DevSecOps, providing a comprehensive overview and actionable guidance for seamlessly embedding security into your development processes.

The philosophy of DevSecOps extends beyond traditional DevOps by advocating for the inclusion of security as a fundamental component throughout the software development lifecycle. In an era where digital threats are increasingly sophisticated and pervasive, integrating security

from the outset is not just wise—it is essential for maintaining the integrity, reliability, and security of software systems.

The journey towards adopting DevSecOps is not merely a shift in technology but a transformation in culture. This book will explore how organizations can break down silos between teams, fostering a collaborative environment where security is everyone's responsibility. Through a mix of theoretical frameworks, practical implementations, and real-world case studies, this guide will provide you with the insights needed to understand and leverage DevSecOps practices effectively.

Whether you are a developer, operations manager, security professional, or business leader, this book will equip you with the knowledge and tools to implement a robust DevSecOps culture in your organization. It is written with the goal of making security a natural and efficient part of your daily workflows, rather than an afterthought or a disruptive barrier to innovation.

As you turn these pages, you will find strategies to enhance collaboration among cross-functional teams, integrate cutting-edge security tools into your CI/CD pipelines, and address common challenges that organizations face while adopting DevSecOps. The aim is to cultivate a security-minded ethos that can anticipate and mitigate risks proactively, ensuring that your software delivery is both rapid and secure.

Thank you for choosing this book as your companion on this vital journey. The principles and practices discussed here are intended to guide you through the evolving landscape of software development, helping your organization not only to survive but to thrive in an ecosystem where security is seamlessly integrated with every code commit.

Let's embark on this transformative journey together, building safer systems that do not compromise on speed or innovation.

# Chapter 1
# Introduction to DevSecOps

# Chapter 1

# Introduction to DevSecOps

In today's fast-paced digital landscape, the integration of security into the development and operational processes of software delivery—known as DevSecOps—has become critical. This chapter provides a foundational understanding of what DevSecOps is, its origins, and its core principles, setting the stage for deeper exploration in subsequent chapters.

## What is DevSecOps?

DevSecOps stands for Development, Security, and Operations. It represents an evolutionary view of the DevOps framework where security is integrated into every phase of the software development lifecycle. DevSecOps aims to embed security as a shared responsibility across the product lifecycle, ensuring that security considerations are not left to the final stages or bolted on after development cycles.

## Historical Context and Evolution

- **From DevOps to DevSecOps**: Initially, the DevOps movement was focused on breaking down silos between development and operations teams to enhance agility and speed in software delivery. However, as security breaches became more frequent and severe, it became evident that security needed to be a fundamental component of this integration, not an optional or final layer.

- **Shift Left Approach**: DevSecOps promotes the 'Shift Left' ideology, which involves introducing security earlier in the development process. This approach helps in identifying and addressing security vulnerabilities during the earliest stages of software development, reducing the cost and complexity of fixes down the line.

## Core Principles of DevSecOps

1. **Automation:** Leveraging tools and technologies to automate security tasks (like static and dynamic code analysis) within the CI/CD pipeline to reduce manual oversight and errors.

2. **Collaboration and Communication**: Encouraging ongoing dialogue between development, security, and operations teams to share insights and best practices.

3. **Continuous Integration and Continuous Delivery (CI/CD):** Integrating security assessments and checks into continuous integration and delivery processes to ensure that every release meets security standards.

4. **Continuous Monitoring**: Implementing real-time monitoring to detect, alert, and respond to security threats immediately.

5. **Security as Code:** Treating security configurations and controls just like application code, which is version-controlled and automated.

## Importance of DevSecOps

- **Enhanced Security Posture:** By integrating security throughout, DevSecOps helps to minimize vulnerabilities and protect against both internal and external threats.

- **Cost Efficiency:** Early detection of security issues significantly reduces the costs associated with post-deployment fixes.

- **Compliance and Trust:** Adhering to regulatory requirements becomes streamlined, and stakeholder trust is enhanced through demonstrable security measures.

- **Resilient Infrastructure**: Continuous security practices lead to more robust and resilient infrastructure, capable of withstanding sophisticated cyber threats.

By embedding security practices at every stage of the software development lifecycle, businesses can not only accelerate their development cycles but also significantly enhance their security frameworks. As we delve deeper into the subsequent chapters, we will explore how to implement these principles effectively, the tools that facilitate this integration, and the cultural shifts necessary to embrace this comprehensive approach.

# Chapter 2
# The Culture of DevSecOps

## Chapter 2

# The Culture of DevSecOps

The successful implementation of DevSecOps requires more than just new tools and processes; it necessitates a fundamental shift in organizational culture. This chapter explores how to build a collaborative culture that not only embraces DevSecOps principles but also promotes security as a shared responsibility within the organization.

## Creating a DevSecOps Culture

1. **Breaking Down Silos:** The traditional silos between development, operations, and security teams must be dismantled. DevSecOps encourages a unified approach where all teams collaborate closely throughout the software development lifecycle.

2. **Security as Everyone's Responsibility**: Shift the mindset from viewing security as a gate kept by a separate team to a shared accountability. Encourage all team members to take an active role in security decision-making and practices.

3. **Open Communication:** Foster an environment of open communication where security concerns are freely shared and discussed. Regular meetings and shared tools can help maintain transparency and keep all team members updated on security issues and practices.

## Key Strategies to Foster a DevSecOps Culture

- **Education and Training**: Regular training sessions to update teams on the latest security threats and best practices are crucial. This includes secure coding practices, threat modeling, and security tools training.

- **Collaborative Tools and Practices**: Utilize tools that facilitate collaboration and visibility across teams. This includes integrated development environments (IDEs) that support security plugins, shared dashboards for monitoring security metrics, and chat tools for real-time communication.

- **Incentives and Rewards:** Recognize and reward contributions to security, such as identifying potential security flaws or innovating on secure development practices. This can help motivate team members to prioritize security in their daily tasks.

## Challenges in Cultivating a DevSecOps Culture

- **Resistance to Change**: Changing an established culture can be challenging. Resistance often comes from not understanding the benefits or fearing that new processes will slow down development.

- **Skill Gaps**: There may be gaps in security knowledge among development or operations teams that need to be addressed through training and hiring practices.

- **Balancing Speed and Security**: Finding the right balance between maintaining agility in development and ensuring thorough security practices is a common challenge.

Creating a culture that supports DevSecOps is a critical step toward achieving more secure software delivery. It requires commitment from all levels of the organization, from executive sponsorship to individual contributors. By fostering an environment that values security as a fundamental component of the development process, organizations can protect their assets more effectively while continuing to innovate and deliver at high speeds.

# Chapter 3
# Key Practices in DevSecOps

# Chapter 3

# Key Practices in DevSecOps

Adopting DevSecOps involves not only cultural changes but also the integration of specific practices that ensure security is considered at every stage of the software development lifecycle. This chapter outlines the key practices that are foundational to a successful DevSecOps implementation.

## Secure Coding Practices

1. **Security as Part of Code Reviews**: Integrate security considerations into the peer review process to catch vulnerabilities early. This includes checking for common security flaws like SQL injections, XSS, and improper error handling.

2. **Education on Secure Coding:** Continuously train developers on secure coding techniques and the latest security threats. Utilize e-learning platforms and in-house workshops to keep knowledge up-to-date.

3. **Use of Standardized Libraries and Frameworks:** Encourage the use of well-maintained libraries and frameworks that adhere to security best practices, reducing the risk of introducing vulnerabilities through custom code.

## Automated Security Testing

1. **Static Application Security Testing (SAST):** Implement tools that analyze source code at rest to detect security vulnerabilities without executing the code.

2. **Dynamic Application Security Testing (DAST):** Use tools that test the running application to find vulnerabilities that manifest during its operation.

3. **Integration into CI/CD Pipeline**: Automate these testing tools within the CI/CD pipeline to ensure that security testing is part of every build and not an afterthought.

## Threat Modeling and Risk Assessment

1. **Regular Threat Modeling Sessions:** Conduct regular sessions to discuss and analyze potential threats specific to each project. This helps teams understand the threat landscape and design more secure systems.

2. **Risk Assessment Procedures:** Establish procedures to assess the risks associated with identified vulnerabilities. This helps prioritize security efforts based on potential impact.

3. **Proactive Rather Than Reactive Security**: Shift from a reactive to a proactive security approach by anticipating potential security issues and addressing them before they become actual vulnerabilities.

## Continuous Monitoring

1. **Real-time Security Monitoring**: Implement monitoring tools that provide real-time insights into the security state of applications and infrastructure. This includes detecting unusual activity that could indicate a security breach.

2. **Feedback Loops:** Create feedback loops where the insights gained from monitoring are used to continuously improve security practices and tooling.

3. **Incident Response Planning**: Develop and regularly update an incident response plan that defines how to respond to security breaches effectively.

## Security as Code

1. **Infrastructure as Code (IaC):** Manage security policies and configurations as code. This ensures consistency and

traceability and integrates security into automated deployment processes.

2. **Policy as Code:** Define security policies in code formats that can be versioned and tracked. This makes it easier to review changes and ensure compliance with security standards.

## Challenges and Solutions

- **Integration Complexity**: Integrating numerous tools and practices into existing systems can be complex. Solutions include incremental integration and choosing tools that complement each other.

 - **Keeping Up with Advancements**: The rapid evolution of technology means that security practices must continually adapt. Ongoing education and engagement with the security community are crucial.

DevSecOps is about embedding security into every aspect of the development process. By adopting these key practices, organizations can ensure that security is a continuous, integrated component of all IT and development activities. This chapter has provided a framework for establishing a robust DevSecOps practice that not only secures software but also enhances the operational and developmental agility of the organization.

# Chapter 4
# Tools and Technologies

## Chapter 4

# Tools and Technologies

Effective DevSecOps implementation relies heavily on the right set of tools and technologies that automate and integrate security processes seamlessly into the software development lifecycle. This chapter provides an overview of key tools and technologies that are essential for executing DevSecOps practices, focusing on how they can enhance both security and operational efficiency.

## Integration of Security Tools into CI/CD Pipelines

1. **Static and Dynamic Analysis Tools:** Incorporate tools like SonarQube for static code analysis and OWASP ZAP for dynamic analysis directly into CI/CD pipelines. This ensures that every

piece of code is automatically scanned for vulnerabilities before it goes into production.

2. **Container Security Tools:** Use tools such as Aqua Security or Twistlock to manage the security of containerized applications, including vulnerability scanning and runtime protection.

3. **Automated Compliance Scanning:** Tools like Chef InSpec or HashiCorp Sentinel can automate compliance checks against predefined security policies during the CI/CD process.

## Securing Containers and Orchestration Platforms

1. **Container Vulnerability Management**: Implement tools that scan container images for known vulnerabilities as part of the build process, such as Clair or Docker Bench for Security.

2. **Orchestration Security**: Secure Kubernetes or other orchestration tools by integrating security auditing tools like Kubernetes Security Posture Management (KSPM) solutions that continuously check for misconfigurations and compliance.

3. **Network Segmentation and Encryption**: Utilize network policies and service meshes like Istio to enforce traffic encryption and micro-segmentation in container environments to limit the blast radius of potential attacks.

## Secure Code Repositories

1. **Branch Protection Rules:** Employ branch protection rules in Git repositories to prevent unauthorized modifications to the code base and ensure that changes are reviewed before merging.

2. **Secrets Management**: Use tools like HashiCorp Vault or AWS Secrets Manager to securely store and manage access to

secrets, API keys, and credentials, ensuring they are not hard-coded in source files.

## Security Orchestration, Automation, and Response (SOAR)

1. **SOAR Tools**: Implement SOAR solutions such as Splunk Phantom or IBM Resilient to automate security incident response workflows and coordinate actions across various security tools.

2. **Custom Integration**: Customize SOAR platforms to integrate with existing tools and workflows, enhancing the overall security response capabilities without disrupting development processes.

## Real-Time Security Monitoring and Analytics

1. **SIEM Solutions**: Use Security Information and Event Management (SIEM) tools like Splunk or LogRhythm to

aggregate logs and monitor data in real time, providing insights into potential security threats.

2. **Behavioral Analytics**: Employ User and Entity Behavior Analytics (UEBA) features within SIEM tools to detect anomalies and potentially malicious activities based on deviations from normal patterns.

## Challenges in Tool Integration

- **Tool Overload**: The challenge of managing multiple tools can lead to reduced effectiveness. Streamlining tools and ensuring they integrate well with each other is crucial.

 - **Skills Gap**: Adequate training and expertise are required to fully leverage these advanced tools. Investing in continuous learning and development is key.

The selection and integration of appropriate DevSecOps tools and technologies are crucial for enhancing the security and efficiency of development and operational workflows. By automating security tasks and ensuring continuous compliance, organizations can not only safeguard their applications but also accelerate their market release cycles. This chapter has equipped you with knowledge about the tools that can help you build a more secure and responsive DevSecOps environment.

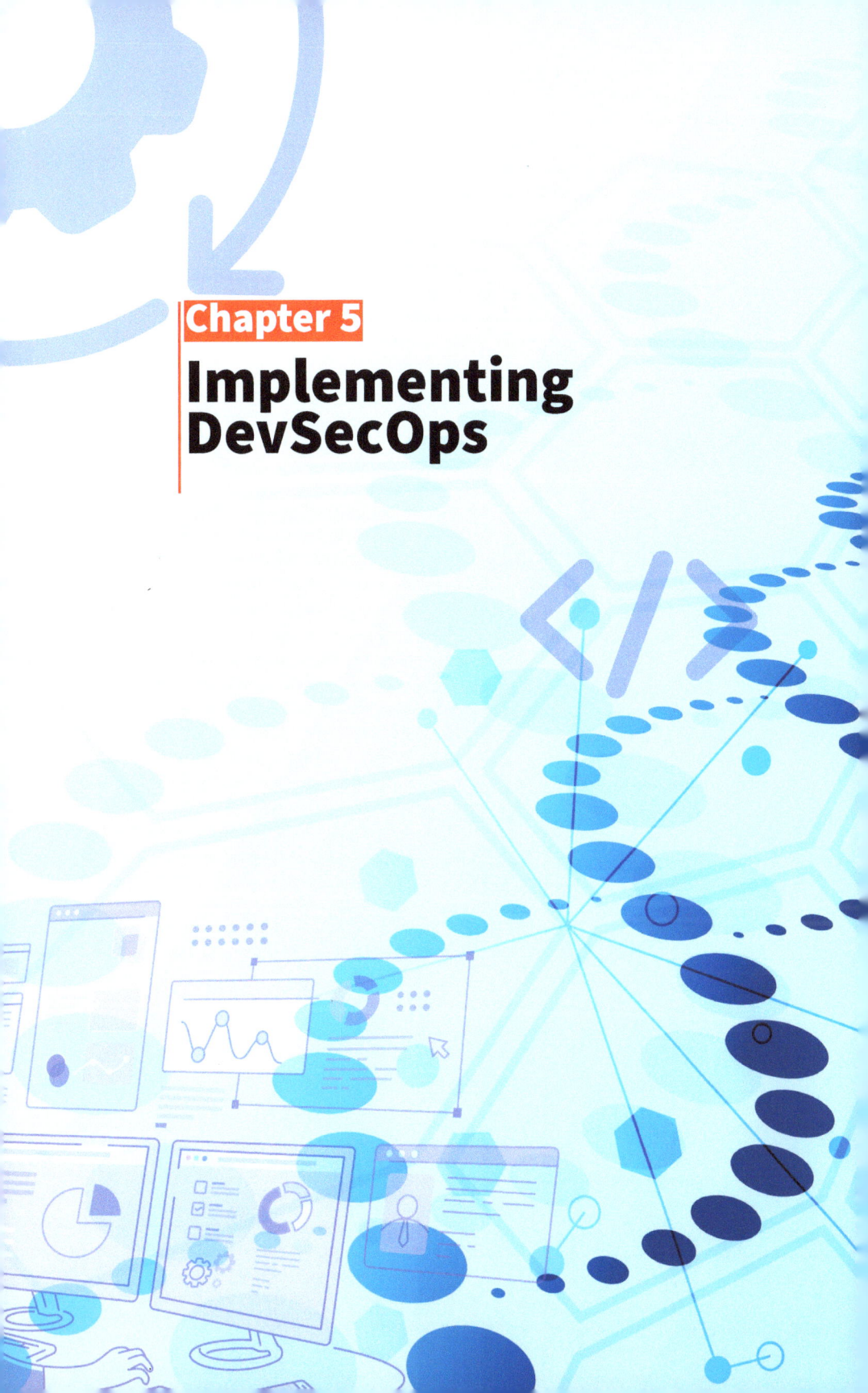

# Chapter 5
# Implementing DevSecOps

# Chapter 5

# Implementing DevSecOps

Transitioning to a DevSecOps model involves strategic planning, tool integration, and ongoing management. This chapter offers a comprehensive guide to successfully implementing DevSecOps in an organization, detailing a step-by-step approach to ensure a smooth and effective transformation.

## Step-by-Step Implementation Guide

**1. Assessment and Planning**

- Current State Analysis: Begin with assessing the current security practices, development processes, and tools in use. Identify gaps where security needs reinforcement.

- Goal Setting: Define clear, measurable goals for what DevSecOps will achieve in terms of security improvements, operational efficiency, and compliance.

2. **Building a Cross-Functional Team**

- Team Composition: Form a cross-functional team that includes members from development, operations, and security to foster collaboration.

- Roles and Responsibilities: Clearly define roles and responsibilities to ensure everyone knows their tasks and how they contribute to the DevSecOps objectives.

3. **Selecting and Integrating Tools**

- Tool Selection: Choose tools that align with your specific security needs and seamlessly integrate with your existing CI/CD pipeline.

- Integration: Integrate these tools into the development process, ensuring they automate security checks without disrupting workflows.

4. **Developing and Implementing Processes**

- Security Integration in SDLC: Integrate security practices at every stage of the software development lifecycle, from initial design to deployment and maintenance.

- Automate Security Practices: Automate as many security processes as possible, such as code scanning and compliance checks, to reduce human error and free up resources for more complex tasks.

5. **Training and Awareness Programs**

- Ongoing Training: Implement regular training sessions to keep the team updated on the latest security threats and DevSecOps practices.

- Awareness Programs: Create awareness programs to ensure that all employees understand the importance of security and their role in maintaining it.

6. **Continuous Monitoring and Feedback**

- Monitoring Systems: Deploy monitoring systems to continuously track the security posture and automatically alert teams about potential issues.

- Feedback Loops: Establish feedback loops to continuously improve the processes based on real-world data and team input.

## Challenges and Mitigation Strategies

- **Cultural Resistance**: Overcome resistance by demonstrating the value of integrated security practices through pilot projects and success stories.

- **Complex Tooling Landscape**: Simplify the tooling landscape by choosing versatile tools that offer multiple functionalities and integrate well with each other.

- **Scaling Issues**: Develop scalable policies and practices that can grow with the organization, ensuring that security does not become a bottleneck.

Implementing DevSecOps is not a one-time project but an ongoing journey that evolves with your organization and the broader security landscape. This chapter provides a roadmap for successfully adopting DevSecOps, emphasizing the importance of collaboration, automation, and continuous improvement. By following these guidelines, organizations can ensure that their development processes are not only efficient but also secure by design.

# Chapter 6
# Challenges and Solutions

# Chapter 6

# Challenges and Solutions

While implementing DevSecOps offers substantial benefits, it also presents unique challenges that organizations must navigate. This chapter discusses common hurdles faced during DevSecOps adoption and provides practical solutions to overcome these obstacles, ensuring a smoother transition and more effective security integration.

## Common Pitfalls in DevSecOps Implementation

1. **Lack of Buy-In**

   - **Challenge**: Resistance from team members or leadership due to lack of understanding of DevSecOps benefits.

- **Solution**: Conduct workshops and presentations to demonstrate the value of DevSecOps, focusing on case studies and industry examples that highlight efficiency gains and security improvements.

2. **Skill Gaps**

   - **Challenge**: Insufficient expertise in new tools or processes, leading to implementation delays or inefficiencies.

   - **Solution**: Invest in training programs and certifications for team members. Consider hiring or contracting specialists with prior DevSecOps experience to bridge immediate gaps.

3. **Tool Integration Issues**

   - **Challenge**: Difficulties in integrating new security tools into existing CI/CD pipelines, causing disruptions or compatibility issues.

- **Solution**: Choose tools with proven compatibility with existing systems or those that offer extensive customization options. Conduct pilot tests to identify and resolve integration issues before full-scale deployment.

4. **Balancing Speed and Security**

- **Challenge**: Maintaining the speed of development cycles while implementing thorough security checks.

- **Solution**: Optimize security testing processes and tools for speed and efficiency. Use automated tools to perform security checks in parallel with development activities.

5. **Advanced Persistent Threats (APTs) and Countermeasures**

- **Understanding APTs**: Advanced Persistent Threats are sophisticated, prolonged cyberattacks that aim to steal information or disrupt operations. They pose a significant risk to organizations, especially those dealing with sensitive or valuable data.

- **Countermeasures**: Implement layered security defenses, conduct regular security audits, and engage in continuous monitoring to detect and respond to unusual activities. Educate employees about the tactics used in APTs, such as social engineering and spear phishing.

## 6. Cultural Adaptation

- **Challenge**: Shifting organizational culture to embrace ongoing security practices as part of daily operations.

- **Solution**: Foster a culture of security by integrating security awareness into the core values of the organization. Recognize and reward contributions to security improvements.

7. **Regulatory Compliance**

- **Challenge**: Adapting DevSecOps practices to meet diverse regulatory requirements, which can vary significantly by industry and region.

- **Solution**: Develop a compliance roadmap that aligns DevSecOps practices with specific regulatory needs. Utilize compliance as code tools to automate and ensure adherence to regulations.

Successfully overcoming the challenges of DevSecOps requires a strategic approach, tailored solutions, and a commitment to continuous improvement. This chapter has provided insights into navigating these challenges, empowering organizations to realize the full potential of DevSecOps and enhance their security posture without sacrificing operational efficiency.

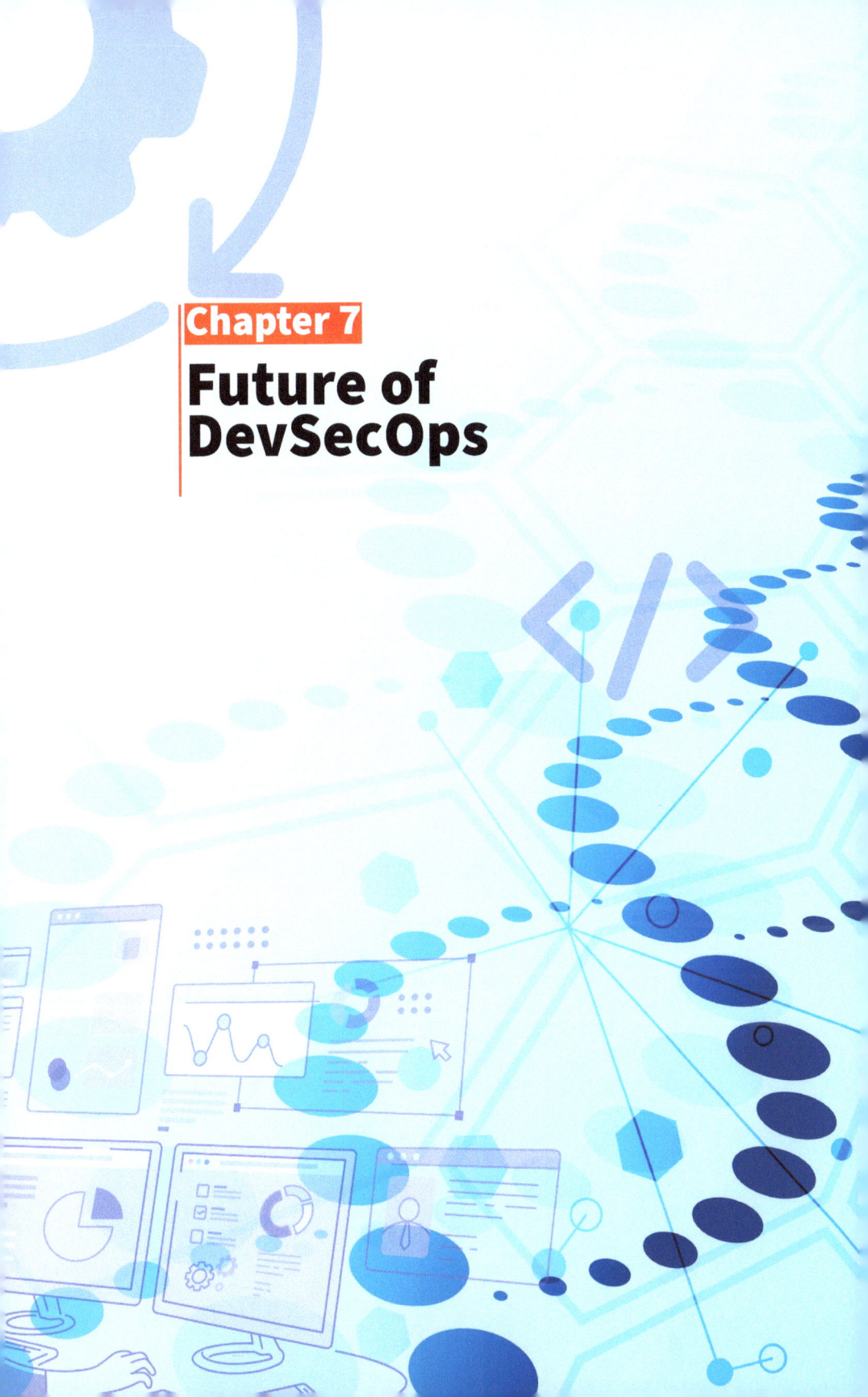

## Chapter 7
# Future of DevSecOps

# Chapter 7

# Future of DevSecOps

As technology continues to advance and cyber threats become more sophisticated, the role of DevSecOps is poised to grow even more critical. This chapter explores the emerging trends and future directions in DevSecOps, highlighting how organizations can prepare to stay ahead in a rapidly evolving digital landscape.

## Emerging Trends in DevSecOps

1. **Artificial Intelligence and Machine Learning**

   - **Usage**: AI and ML are increasingly being integrated into DevSecOps to automate complex decision-making processes, such as threat detection and response.

- **Impact**: These technologies can significantly reduce response times to security incidents and help predict potential vulnerabilities before they are exploited.

2. **Increased Automation**

  - **Trend**: There is a move towards even greater automation of security processes, aiming to achieve near-real-time security assurance throughout the development lifecycle.

  - **Benefits**: Automation helps maintain the speed of DevOps while ensuring that security is tightly integrated without causing delays.

3. **Shift Towards Developer Security Operations (DevSecOps)**

  - **Evolution**: Developers are being equipped with tools and training to take on more security responsibilities, a trend sometimes referred to as shifting left even further.

- **Advantages**: This shift empowers developers to fix security issues in real-time, significantly enhancing the security of delivered software.

## Scalability and Evolution of DevSecOps

- **Scalable Architectures**: As organizations grow, their DevSecOps architectures must scale accordingly. This involves using cloud-native security tools and services that can dynamically adjust based on the load and threat landscape.

- **Continuous Learning and Adaptation**: DevSecOps teams must continually update their skills and tools to handle new security challenges and technological advancements.

## Challenges and Future Considerations

- **Complexity Management**: As DevSecOps tools and processes become more sophisticated, managing this complexity without overwhelming the team or compromising the agility of development becomes crucial.

- **Integration of Emerging Technologies**: Integrating new technologies, such as 5G and IoT, into the DevSecOps framework poses challenges due to their novel security vulnerabilities.

The future of DevSecOps is promising yet demands vigilance and adaptability. Organizations must stay informed about technological advancements and evolving cyber threats to continuously refine their DevSecOps strategies. By embracing change and fostering a culture of innovation within security practices, businesses can protect their assets more effectively and sustain their competitive edge in the digital age.

# Chapter 8
# DevSecOps & Cloud-Native

## Chapter 8

# Integrating DevSecOps with Cloud-Native Technologies

As organizations shift towards cloud-native architectures, integrating security into every aspect of software development and operations has never been more critical. This chapter delves into the complexities of cloud-native technologies, such as Kubernetes, serverless, and microservices, and explores strategies to implement DevSecOps effectively in these environments.

## Cloud-Native Security Fundamentals

**Cloud-Native Architectures Defined**: Cloud-native technologies leverage scalable, distributed architectures that consist of containers, microservices, and serverless functions. These technologies foster agility but introduce new security challenges due to their dynamic and ephemeral nature.

**Core Security Challenges**: The main challenges include managing scalable security configurations, enforcing consistent security policies across diverse environments, and securing inter-service communications. Identity and access management, data encryption, and network segmentation are paramount in cloud-native settings.

## DevSecOps in Kubernetes Environment

**Securing Container Orchestrations**: Kubernetes, the de facto standard for orchestrating containers, requires rigorous security practices. Implementing network policies, pod security policies, and role-based access control (RBAC) can help secure Kubernetes clusters.

**Integrating Security into CI/CD Pipelines**: Automating security checks within Kubernetes workflows using tools like Helm

charts for package management and Skaffold for continuous development can ensure that security is baked into the infrastructure from the start.

## Serverless Security Practices

**Unique Vulnerabilities of Serverless**: Serverless architectures reduce the attack surface by eliminating the need to manage servers but introduce specific vulnerabilities such as event injection and insecure serverless deployment configurations.

**Applying DevSecOps Principles**: Security in serverless architectures can be integrated by automating role management through infrastructure as code (IaC) and applying principle of least privilege to function executions.

## Securing Microservices

**Microservices Security Design**: Designing microservices with security in mind involves implementing encrypted data flows, mutual TLS for service authentication, and fine-grained authorization controls.

**Decentralized Security Management**: Each microservice should implement its own set of security controls, which can be managed through centralized policies distributed via a service mesh like Istio.

## Tools and Technologies

**Cloud-Native Security Tools**: Tools such as Aqua Security for container security, Sysdig Secure for runtime security, and Prisma Cloud for posture management are essential in maintaining the security of cloud-native applications.

**Automation and Orchestration Tools**: Leveraging tools like Terraform for IaC and Ansible for configuration management can help automate the deployment of security controls at scale.

## Future Trends in Cloud-Native DevSecOps

**Evolving Threat Landscape**: As technology evolves, so do the threats. This section will explore how emerging technologies such as AI and machine learning are being leveraged to automate threat detection and response in cloud-native environments.

**Continuous Improvement Strategies**: The need for agile and adaptive security practices that evolve with new technologies and threat vectors is crucial. This section will outline strategies for maintaining an effective security posture through continuous improvement and learning.

Integrating DevSecOps within cloud-native technologies is not merely a technical challenge but a strategic necessity. By adopting the practices and tools discussed in this chapter, organizations can enhance their security posture while benefiting from the agility and scalability that cloud-native architectures offer.

**CONCLUSION** 2024

WWW.MOHAMEDFAWZI.NET

# DEVSECOPS FOR CONTINUOUS INNOVATION

# Conclusion

As we reach the conclusion of " DevSecOps for Continuous Innovationit" is clear that the integration of security into every phase of the software development and operations process is not just a best practice but a necessity in today's digital world. This book has guided you through the foundational principles of DevSecOps, the cultural shifts required, the key practices, the essential tools, and the comprehensive strategies needed to implement these changes effectively within your organization.

From the initial chapters that laid the groundwork in understanding DevSecOps, to the detailed discussions on the necessary tools and practices, this journey has been about transforming how we think about and handle security in technology development. We've explored how automating security tasks and embedding them early in the development cycle does not just mitigate risks but also enhances operational efficiency and product integrity.

## Reflecting on Key Insights:

- **Culture is Crucial**: The success of DevSecOps hinges not just on technology but on people. Cultivating a culture that embraces security as a collective responsibility is foundational.

- **Continuous Improvement**: DevSecOps is not a set-it-and-forget-it solution. It requires continuous assessment, adaptation, and improvement as technologies evolve and threat landscapes change.

- **Collaboration and Communication**: Breaking down silos and fostering open communication between development, operations, and security teams are essential for the proactive identification and management of security issues.

As technology continues to advance and the frequency and sophistication of cyber threats increase, the principles of DevSecOps will become even more integral to the development process. The future of software development is one where security and development are not just aligned but integrated, with each new line of code evaluated for both functionality and security.

## Looking Forward:

Embrace the changes and challenges as opportunities for growth and improvement. Encourage your teams to innovate with security in mind, and continue to invest in the tools and training that will equip them to succeed. The path to integrating DevSecOps may vary between organizations, but the destination—a secure, efficient, and compliant operational environment—is universal.

**CASE STUDY** 2024
WWW.MOHAMEDFAWZI.NET

# DEVSECOPS FOR CONTINUOUS INNOVATION

# Comprehensive Case Study

## ISD Software Solutions

## Overview

As the CISO at ISD, I oversee our technology company specializing in developing sophisticated software solutions for remote alarms, monitoring, and situational awareness. Faced with escalating cyber threats and the imperative to preserve our competitive advantage in the rapidly progressing tech landscape, we strategically decided to adopt DevSecOps practices across our development and operations teams. This initiative is aimed at enhancing our security measures seamlessly throughout our software development lifecycle, ensuring robust defense mechanisms are in place as we continue to innovate and lead in our field.

## Situation

Traditionally, ISD's development and operations approach was becoming insufficient to handle the complexities of modern cybersecurity threats and the rapid deployment demands of our industry.

## Action

We adopted the DevSecOps framework to integrate security deeply and seamlessly into every stage of our software development lifecycle, starting from initial design through development, deployment, and maintenance.

## Challenge

Initially, there was resistance from developers and operations teams due to a lack of understanding and the perceived additional workload of integrating security into their daily tasks.

## Solution

To address this, ISD's management, including myself, conducted workshops and interactive sessions to educate all stakeholders about the benefits of DevSecOps, focusing on how it could streamline workflows and enhance security. We also introduced incentives for successfully meeting security benchmarks.

## Implementation

- **Secure Coding Practices**: We integrated secure coding training into our development process, making it mandatory for all software developers.

- **Automated Security Testing**: We incorporated static and dynamic application security testing tools into our CI/CD pipeline to detect vulnerabilities early.

- **Continuous Monitoring**: Deployed real-time monitoring tools to keep track of security issues in development and production environments.

## Tools Deployed

- **SAST and DAST Tools**: Tools like SonarQube and OWASP ZAP were integrated into our development pipelines.

- **Container Security**: Utilized Aqua Security to manage and secure our Docker containers and Kubernetes orchestration.

- **SOAR Solutions**: Implemented IBM Resilient to automate the response to security incidents, ensuring quick and efficient handling.

## Implementing DevSecOps

1. **Assessment of Current Practices**: I evaluated our existing security practices and identified gaps.

2. **Cross-Functional Teams**: Formed teams that included members from development, operations, and security to foster collaboration.

3. **Regular Reviews and Adaptations**: Instituted a routine of continuous feedback and iterative improvements to refine processes.

## Complexity Management

- **Challenge**: The integration of multiple new tools led to complexity and initial operational challenges.

- **Solution**: We streamlined our toolchain by selecting versatile tools that offered broad functionality, reducing overlap, and simplifying training needs.

## Future-Proofing

- **Challenge**: Keeping up with the rapidly evolving tech landscape and emerging security threats.

- **Solution**: I established a dedicated innovation team within the DevSecOps unit to focus on emerging technologies and cybersecurity trends.

## Preparation for Future Challenges

- **AI and ML Integration**: We began exploring AI-driven security tools to predict vulnerabilities and automate threat detection.

- **Scaling DevSecOps**: Developed plans to ensure our DevSecOps practices could scale with the company's growth, leveraging cloud-native solutions and automated scalability checks.

## Conclusion

Through the strategic implementation of DevSecOps, we enhanced not only our security posture but also our overall operational efficiency and product quality. This comprehensive approach allowed ISD to maintain leadership in our industry, ensuring that our software solutions remain secure, reliable, and ahead of the curve in meeting the needs of our customers.

**2024**

**AUTHOR**

WWW.MOHAMEDFAWZI.NET

# DEVSECOPS FOR CONTINUOUS INNOVATION

**Mohamed Fawzi Elgendi**
**www.fawzooz.ai**

# Mohamed Fawzi Elgendi

me@mohamedfawzi.net
Dubai, UAE

**AI Enthusiast & Mental wellness Author**

Pioneering Digital Innovation, AI Advancement, Information Security, and Promoting Mental Wellness.

**Chief Information Security Officer (CISO)**

**Chief Digital and AI Officer (CDAO)**

**Post Graduate Program in Artificial Intelligence For Leaders**

**Bachelor's degree in Computer and Systems Engineering**

**400+** Mentee
**70+** Project
**17+** Book
**16Y+** Experience

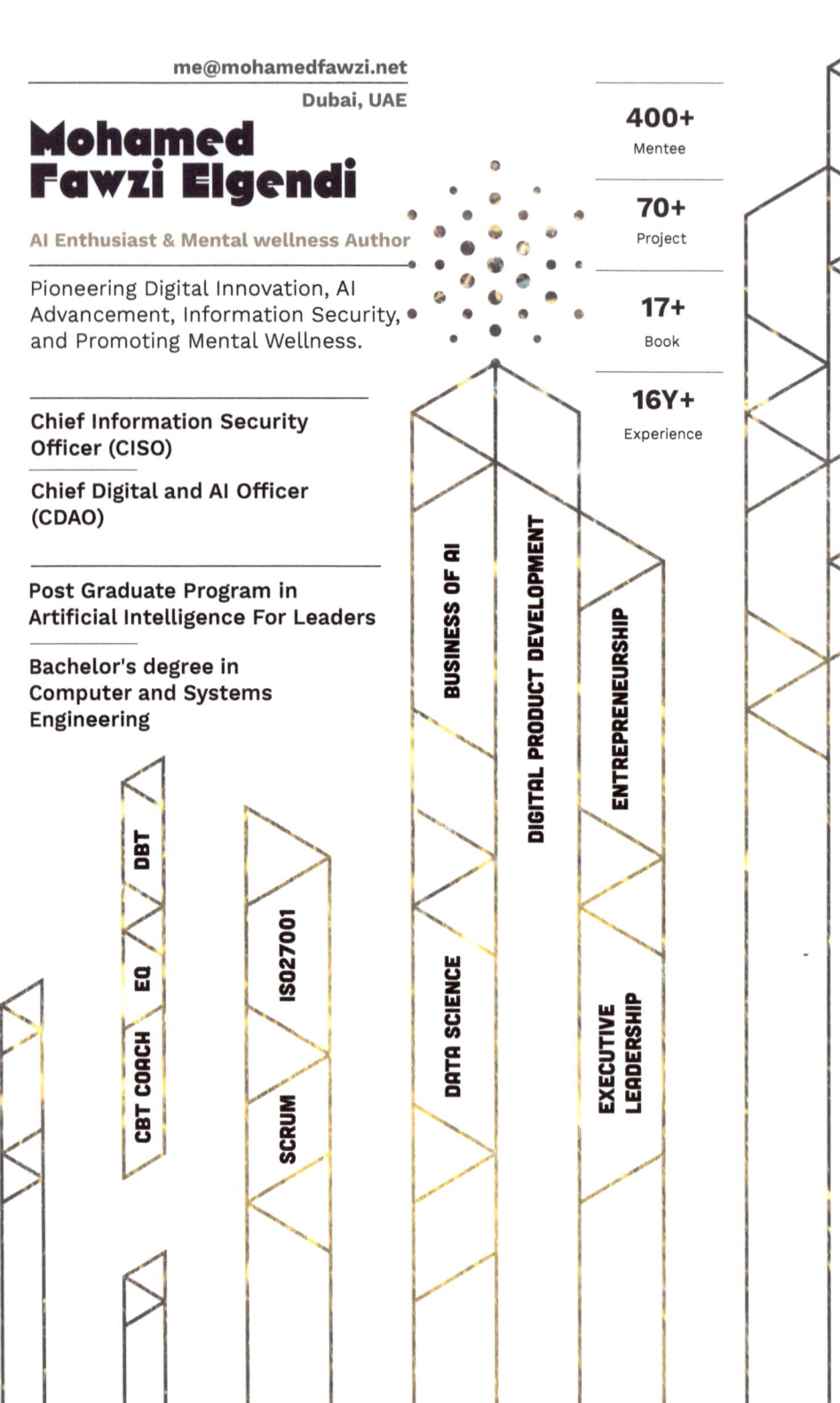

- DBT
- EQ
- CBT COACH
- ISO27001
- SCRUM
- DATA SCIENCE
- BUSINESS OF AI
- DIGITAL PRODUCT DEVELOPMENT
- ENTREPRENEURSHIP
- EXECUTIVE LEADERSHIP

www.ingramcontent.com/pod-product-compliance
Lightning Source LLC
Chambersburg PA
CBHW040229220526
45473CB00001B/169